W9-AWQ-510

Your Carbon Footprint™

Reducing Your Carbon Footprint
at School

Jeanne Nagle

rosen publishing's
rosen
central

New York

For Jody

Published in 2009 by The Rosen Publishing Group, Inc.
29 East 21st Street, New York, NY 10010

First Edition

Library of Congress Cataloging-in-Publication Data

Nagle, Jeanne.
Your carbon footprint: reducing your carbon footprint at school / Jeanne Nagle.
    p. cm.
Includes bibliographical references and index.
ISBN-13: 978-1-4042-1774-4 (library binding)
1. Automobiles—Motors—Exhaust gas—Environmental aspects—Juvenile literature.
2. Atmospheric carbon dioxide—Juvenile literature. 3. Global warming—Juvenile literature. I. Title.

TD886.5.N33 2008
640—dc22

2008000678

Manufactured in the United States of America

On the cover: Clockwise, from upper left: Recycling containers; a student in Earth science class; students recover used vegetable oil from their school cafeteria for use in a biodiesel project.

Contents

Introduction

On October 12, 2007, former U.S. vice president Al Gore and the United Nations Intergovernmental Panel on Climate Change together received the Nobel Peace Prize. This special honor put a well-deserved spotlight on important ecological issues. What Gore and the panel have been investigating is the effect of human activity on the world's climate. Of special concern is global warming, which involves a slow but steady increase in the temperature of Earth's surface and its oceans.

Energy from the sun (solar energy) enters Earth's atmosphere and becomes heat (infrared energy). Gases in the atmosphere, including carbon dioxide, let sunlight through to warm the land and oceans, but then they act like a blanket to trap the infrared energy as it radiates back out into space. This is what is known as the greenhouse effect.

The greenhouse effect is a natural process necessary for the survival of all living things on Earth. However, when too much carbon dioxide and other greenhouse gases are present in the atmosphere, they can knock the system out of balance. As the gases build up, more heat gets trapped here on Earth, causing temperatures to rise unnaturally. Rising temperatures change the planet's climate and can cause all sorts of problems, including an increase in weather-related disasters such as hurricanes.

Gore and the UN scientists believe climate change is happening right now, and they also believe that human activities producing carbon dioxide and other gases are a major cause of the problem. In other words, people are contributing to higher carbon dioxide levels in the atmosphere. Scientists call the amount of carbon we produce our "carbon footprint."

Fortunately, each of us can take action to reduce the size of the carbon footprints we leave on the planet. All it takes is some creative thinking and the willingness to make some relatively minor lifestyle changes. You may wonder how one person can make a difference. Working by yourself or within a group, you can make a difference at home, in your town, or, as this book will show, at school.

Out and About

Whether you realize it or not, you leave a pretty big carbon footprint at school. The activities that release carbon emissions don't take place just in the classroom. In fact, greenhouse gas contributions start even before you and your classmates and teachers enter the building. For example, the way people choose to get to and from school makes an impact, as does how the school grounds are managed and maintained.

Impact of Transportation

The burning of fossil fuels is the biggest contributor to human-produced greenhouse gases. Fossil fuels were created from the remains of ancient animals and plants. They include coal, oil, and oil's by-product, petroleum (gasoline). Gasoline is burned to run cars and other vehicles, making driving one of the main ways that individuals leave their carbon footprint on the planet.

The cars, trucks, and sport utility vehicles (SUVs) that Americans drive for their personal use gobble up two-thirds of the fuel set aside for transportation in the United States. The exhaust that comes as a result of burning fuel in these vehicles makes up about one-third of the country's total carbon dioxide production, which is estimated at a whopping 1,600 million metric tons each year. By way of comparison, passenger vehicles in Europe are estimated to be responsible for just over one-tenth of that continent's human-produced CO_2, according to figures compiled by the European Commission in 2004. In fact, the nonprofit advocacy group Environmental Defense states that the total carbon emissions of passenger vehicles in the United States is greater than the total carbon emissions of most countries. It only makes sense, then, that the environment is better off when you make fewer trips in the family car.

Alternative Ways to Travel

The two best ways to help reduce carbon emissions are attached to the bottoms of your legs—your feet. Walking is the form of transportation that has the least negative impact on the environment. In other words, tracks made with your feet result in an overall smaller carbon footprint. An added bonus is that walking is great exercise and can make you healthier.

Riding a bike, skateboard, or foot-powered scooter are considered the second-best transportation methods when it comes to reducing your carbon footprint. The process of making bicycles, skateboards, and scooters and then shipping them to stores causes carbon dioxide and other pollutants to be released into the atmosphere. But riding them emits none, just like walking. Also just like walking, riding your bike or skateboard to and from school gets your heart pumping and is better for you than being driven in a car.

If it is too far or dangerous for you to walk to school, or the weather doesn't allow you to ride your bike or skateboard, consider a car pool. For this arrangement, several students who live near each other ride together to and from school, potentially reducing the number of cars on the road.

Another option is public transportation. This may be easiest in big cities, where there are more options, such as trolleys, subways, and trains. However, even smaller towns frequently offer some kind of bus service. The American Public Transportation Association estimates that nearly fourteen million tons of carbon dioxide are kept out of the atmosphere each year as a result of people in the United States taking the bus or subway instead of personal-use vehicles.

Walking and riding a bike are two environmentally friendly and healthy ways to get to and from school.

The Pluses (and Minuses) of School Buses

Every day, some twenty-four million American students take the bus to school. This is good because more people on the bus means that there are fewer who have to be driven in separate cars. Fewer cars out on the road burning fossil fuel means less carbon dioxide is being released into the atmosphere.

The black carbon in the exhaust that is emitted by older school buses is a danger to your lungs as well as the environment.

There is a problem with this solution, though. A majority of school buses run on diesel fuel and emit soot, known as "black carbon," which is hundreds of times stronger—and therefore more dangerous—than CO_2.

If you are committed to taking the bus as a way to limit dangerous gas emissions, go the extra mile and investigate the school buses that operate in your district. If they are older models—and many of the school buses on the road are—suggest that the school district look into ways to curb harmful bus emissions.

Replacing older buses with newer ones that meet standards set by the federal Environmental Protection Agency (EPA) is one way to address the issue. That can be expensive, however. Since 2004, the EPA has required that all new diesel vehicles, including school buses, be equipped with pollution controls such as carbon filtering. Fortunately, there are less costly steps, explained in detail here, that can be taken.

Retrofitting

Retrofitting involves placing (fitting) new technology on old (retro) machinery to make it work better. In the case of school buses, mechanical devices are added to bus engines and exhaust systems to make them more environmentally friendly.

For instance, a diesel oxidation catalyst is a device that uses safe chemicals to break down a vehicle's exhaust pollutants. Diesel oxidation catalysts are less expensive and easier to install than diesel particulate filters, which clean dangerous chemicals out of bus exhaust as it passes from the engine to the tailpipe.

Your school may be concerned about taking such steps because of the expense involved. There may be a way for you to help. Organizations such as the EPA (www.epa.gov) offer grants so that schools can afford retrofits or new buses. Working with a teacher, a school librarian, or your parents, you can find out what grants are available, see what needs to be done to apply, and then help write and send in the application.

Alternative Fuels

Another strategy is to use alternative fuels—such as biodiesel—that give off fewer harmful emissions. Biodiesel is a renewable fuel made from vegetable oils or animal fat. Standard diesel bus engines can run on fuel blended with small amounts of biodiesel without any retrofits. For example, buses in suburban Chicago started using a blended fuel that's part soybean oil and part petroleum in 2005. So far, the move has reduced the exhaust emissions of 1,400 buses by about 25 percent. Communities in Maine, West Virginia, Nevada, Kentucky, and New Jersey have had similar success with biodiesel school buses.

Better Driving Practices

Finally, you can lead the effort to get school bus drivers to agree to a low-idle plan. When an engine idles, or runs without the vehicle moving, it is still producing harmful emissions. Turning off bus engines during extended loading and unloading periods reduces emissions. Less idling also saves gas, which saves money.

Landscaping and Groundskeeping

Caring for the grass, plants, and flowers on school grounds may also release greenhouse gases into the atmosphere. The gas- or diesel-powered engines of most landscaping equipment emit carbon exhaust like a car. Moreover, fertilizers and pest sprays frequently contain chemicals such as nitrous oxide, which can add to the problem.

You can help reduce the damage done to the environment by lawn and plant care. First, investigate which plants are native, or grow naturally, in your area. Native vegetation is used to the soil and weather around your school, so it won't need lots of toxic chemicals or extra water to stay healthy. Then approach your teacher or the school principal with

Planting trees and other vegetation on school property is a win-win situation. Carbon dioxide gets filtered out of the air, and the grounds get beautified.

your research in hand. Explain why using native plants on school grounds is important, and suggest that the groundskeepers use native plants in the school's landscaping. To sweeten the deal, you can even volunteer to help plant and care for the new foliage.

Next, suggest that the grass not be cut too often. Fewer mowing sessions translates to less fumes and exhaust. Also, check with the maintenance crew at your school to see if lawn mowers, snowblowers, and other such equipment is regularly cleaned and maintained. Machines in good working order use less fuel and therefore spew less pollution into the air. If possible, volunteer to perform manual tasks, like raking and shoveling, to eliminate the need for electric or gas-powered tools that accomplish the same work.

Finally, you can plant a tree or garden on school grounds. Grass, flowers, trees, and other plant life act as natural filters, soaking up carbon dioxide in the atmosphere and releasing oxygen.

Writing Campaigns

Go to www.house.gov/writerep to find out how to contact your senators and representatives in Congress. Then write letters to encourage them to create effective climate change policy. Taking small, everyday steps to reduce your personal carbon footprint can help quite a bit, but letting your government know that climate change policy is a priority for you is really powerful. You may not be able to vote yet, but there are still ways to get your voice heard.

2 In the Classroom

Usually when you're in class at school, you are the one doing the learning. When it comes to reducing your school's carbon footprint, however, you may find yourself in the position of being the teacher. You can show, tell, and lead by example as you share with your classmates and teachers the possible ways they can lessen their impact on the environment simply by making a few changes in the classroom.

Fossil Fuels and Power Generation

Electricity used to light your classroom, power electronic equipment, and run air conditioners inside the school building is generated by power plants. About half of the electricity consumed in the United States is generated at power plants that burn coal, a fossil fuel. Natural gas and oil account for another 12 percent of U.S. power plant production. When these fossil fuels are burned, they release carbon dioxide and other dangerous chemicals into the air. To reduce the amount of greenhouse gases that get trapped in the atmosphere, we need to reduce our electricity use as well as our coal, oil, and gas consumption.

Schools trying to reduce energy usage could follow the example of Amity Elementary in Boise, Idaho. Amity uses solar energy and earth cover to regulate building temperatures.

Energy Audits

With their outdated lighting systems and modern electronic equipment, many American classrooms are guilty of unnecessary energy use. To figure out where the energy thieves are in your school, you can conduct research called an energy audit. By investigating how your school uses energy, you'll see where it is being wasted.

A representative of your local utility company can do an audit at little or no cost, but where's the fun in that? With help from your classmates and the cooperation of teachers and administrators, you can conduct a simple energy audit in your classroom or throughout the entire school.

First, think about all the ways your school uses energy. Then walk around and take notes on how efficiently energy is used by those sources. For each room you are auditing, make a list of all the appliances and equipment that require electricity, natural gas, or oil—in other words, fossil fuel–based resources—to operate.

For classrooms and offices, you should include the number and types of lights, computers, printers, photocopiers, and audio-visual equipment. Basically, anything that plugs into an outlet should be noted. The school's furnace or boiler, hot-water tanks, and air-conditioning system should also be checked to see how much energy they consume, their condition, and when they were last serviced. If doors and windows rattle, or if you can feel a draft coming from them, then heat and air-conditioning are escaping, and energy is being wasted.

To get a true picture of your school's energy use, remember to factor in usage during all times of the day. That includes before and after school, as well as overnight and during vacations and breaks. Energy consumption will be lower during these times (the heat will be turned down; fewer lights will be on), but there will be some usage.

Tackling the Energy Hogs

The list you make for your audit will reveal where energy is being misused or wasted. Once you pinpoint the areas of concern, you can suggest specific ways to fix the problems. There are some common energy hogs in just about every classroom, including:

Using incandescent lightbulbs shines a spotlight on wasted energy. Switching to compact fluorescent bulbs saves your school money as well as energy.

- **Incandescent lighting.** Because they are inexpensive, traditional incandescent lightbulbs are used by many schools. Unfortunately, only about 10 percent of the energy used by incandescent bulbs produces light, while the remaining 90 percent simply gives off heat. Newer compact fluorescent bulbs are more than four times as efficient. Although they're more expensive, they also last much longer. In the long run, your school will save money by making the switch to compact fluorescent lighting.

- **Electronic equipment.** Electronics such as computers and printers left in stand-by or sleep mode continue to suck up energy. It's better to turn these machines off completely. Unplugging equipment from outlets saves even more energy.

- **Air infiltration.** For various reasons, many school buildings have cracks and holes in the walls, and doors and windows with gaps. All of these situations allow outside air to infiltrate, or come inside. When cold air leaks into the building in the winter, or hot air gets in when you have the air-conditioning running, energy is being wasted. To help avoid infiltration, your school maintenance crew can replace broken window-panes, use inexpensive weather stripping on loose doors and windows, and repair cracks with caulk.

- **HVAC systems.** Heating, ventilation, and cooling (HVAC) systems are responsible for about half of a school's total energy usage. Reducing the amount of energy HVAC systems use would significantly cut your school's energy bills. School administrators should make sure equipment is kept clean and in good working order. Pipes and ducts located in unused or rarely used spaces, like large storage closets, should be wrapped with insulation material. Maintenance workers or an outside heating and cooling expert should check to see if there are any streaks of dirt on furnace ducts or air-conditioning units, especially on seams, where parts are joined together. Grime concentrated in these areas can indicate air leaks. A quick fix for this is to seal all seams with duct tape. A more permanent fix is for the administration to make the switch to energy-efficient furnaces and air-conditioning units, especially if any of the HVAC-related operating units are fifteen years old or older.

The Paper Trail

The materials you use every day in the classroom also have an effect on how large your carbon footprint is. Something as simple as a piece

Fumes from a mill's smokestacks add to the carbon footprint left behind during the paper-making process. Recycling paper reduces energy consumption as well as air pollution.

of paper makes a difference. The energy-intensive steps involved in producing paper—from cutting down trees, to powering paper mills, to transporting the finished products—make the paper industry the third-largest energy-consuming industry in North America.

Look for solutions to paper issues. Visit the Web site of your local school district and search for the purchasing or procurement department. Take down the name of the department's director, as well as his or her phone number and the mailing address for the department. With help from your teacher or parents, write a letter expressing your concern about the paper used at your school. Politely request that the department consider purchasing paper products made with recycled materials. Buying paper with a high percentage of recycled, post-consumer material goes a long way toward reducing your school's carbon footprint. The EPA reports that recycled paper products use around 64 percent less energy to produce, and they leave behind nearly 75 percent less pollution.

Earth-Friendly School Supplies

Once you've taken the time to get notebooks with environmentally friendly recycled paper, you'll need a way to write in them and carry them from class to class that is just as ecologically responsible. Luckily, there are "green" school supplies that will do the job.

As an alternative to disposable ballpoint pens and wood pencils, you can write with less wasteful implements. Refillable pens and mechanical pencils contain either a tube of ink or a thin rod of graphite (pencil lead) that you replace when it is finished. The reusable shells are available in fancy metal versions or relatively inexpensive plastic. Some writing implements are even biodegradable, which means the substances used to make them can be broken down naturally and won't hang around forever in landfills.

Pencils and pens can be made out of recycled materials. Other school products that use recycled materials include binders made out of reused cardboard instead of nonbiodegradable plastic, and sturdy backpacks and book bags created using recycled shopping bags, old tires, and leftover aluminum.

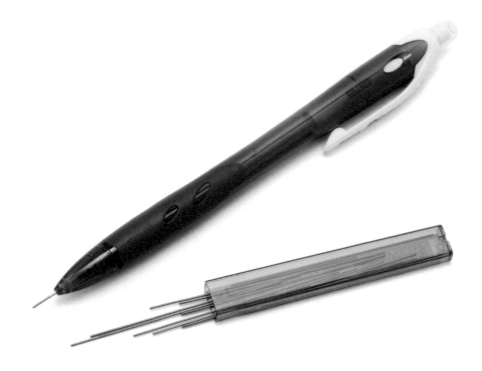

Mechanical pencils look like ballpoint pens but write like a number-two pencil. Their thin, replaceable leads are environmentally friendly—and never need sharpening.

Just as the manufacturers of these and other school products get creative when they figure out how to recycle material, you can find unique uses for items that otherwise might be considered waste. For instance, kids in the lower grades at your school can reuse empty Styrofoam egg holders and packaging materials such as bubble wrap for art projects. Another idea is to clean out nonrecyclable plastic containers and put them to work storing and organizing supplies. The options are limited only by your imagination.

3 | In the Cafeteria

If you're looking for a spot where your school can make a huge difference in the size of its carbon footprint, look no further than the cafeteria. School dining areas use an enormous amount of energy and produce vast quantities of waste.

Food and Greenhouse Gases

From start to finish, the food cycle is full of ecological concerns. First, there is the process of planting, growing, raising, and harvesting what we eat. Clearing the land of carbon-dioxide–filtering trees and plants, releasing carbon left in the soil by dead plants through plowing, emissions from tractors and other machinery, toxic chemicals in pesticides and fertilizer, and methane created by animal manure all contribute to the problem.

Second, there is the fossil fuel energy used to process, package, and ship the food served in cafeterias. Before this food reaches your lunch tray, it is cleaned; processed; boxed, jarred, or canned; and trucked or flown to your location.

Next, there is the energy used to refrigerate, prepare, warm, and cook the food. Industrial kitchens such as the one

School cafeterias are typically large and have long hours of operation, making them prime locations for energy waste.

in your cafeteria often use large refrigerators and stoves, microwaves, toasters, and warming trays and lights. The amount of energy used by these industrial appliances is considerable. The problem is made worse because many cafeterias have older appliances, rather than more recent, energy-efficient models. Also, because waves of people eat meals at different times of the day, the cafeteria must keep cooked food warm for hours, using excess energy for extended periods.

The people in charge may not go for that idea, however, so you should be prepared with other options. These could include having cafeteria staff keep refrigerators as fully stocked as possible and letting hot leftovers cool to room temperature before refrigerating. Coolers work more efficiently when they are full, and hot foods cause the temperature inside the fridge to rise, making the appliance work harder and use up more energy to keep items chilled.

Also, cafeteria workers should make sure appliances are in good working order. They can start by regularly cleaning and vacuuming a refrigerator's compressor coils, located in the back and usually behind a grille near the floor in front. Stoves should be cleaned and maintained as well, and workers should bake or heat several items at the same time whenever possible. Like refrigerators, ovens work best when fully loaded. Dishwashers clean better and use less water if dishes are prerinsed with cold water.

Another good idea is to observe the customer flow in the cafeteria for a week, noting when it seems to be busiest and when the rush slows down. This will give you a general timetable on which you can base a recommended energy-use schedule. For instance, if cooks know when they won't be serving many people, they can either turn down or turn off griddles, stovetop burners, display lights, and warming trays.

Start a Food Waste Program

A tremendous amount of food goes to waste in the United States. To give you an idea of how great the problem is, take a look at a case study conducted by one California school system in 2004. Eight elementary schools in the Davis Joint Unified School District each dumped an average of 9.2 tons of food waste each year. That's about the same weight as one and a half adult male African elephants! Your school would likely post similar numbers.

You can significantly decrease your school's carbon footprint by starting a food waste program. As you did when you tracked your school's energy use, you begin with observation. A food waste audit provides you with detailed information about how much food is going to waste and the best way to get rid of the waste.

Use the Food Waste Hierarchy

The EPA has come up with a food waste hierarchy, meaning it has ranked food waste options from most preferred to least preferred. At the top of the hierarchy is source reduction. This is where you find ways to decrease the amount of food waste you produce. For instance, if you discover that certain foods are not favorites and are constantly being thrown out, you should suggest that the cafeteria not offer those items anymore, or at least offer them less often.

Next in the hierarchy is feeding people. Leftover food that meets quality and safety standards set by the U.S. Department of Agriculture (USDA) can be donated to food banks, soup kitchens, shelters, and food recovery programs such as America's Second Harvest. You can call the National Hunger Clearinghouse at (800) 453-2648 to find out where you can donate excess food in your area.

After feeding people, consider feeding the animals. Some farmers take food scraps to feed their livestock, and zoos might be able to use

Monitoring the recycling of food waste isn't always a pleasant job, but it's necessary to ensure that edible scraps go to the proper place.

certain leftovers. There are laws about feeding food waste to animals, so contact your county agricultural extension office or health department to find out what you can and cannot give to animals.

Further down in the hierarchy is using food waste for industrial purposes, which is known as rendering. Fat, grease, and oil can be separated from other food waste and processed to make biodiesel fuel, as well as soap and cosmetics.

Composting involves letting food scraps naturally decompose to form a rich fertilizer for gardens and landscaping. Place food waste such as fruits and vegetables, egg shells, and coffee grounds in a heap in a contained outdoor area or bin, preferably in a dry, shady spot. (Certain foods, like meat and dairy products, should not be added because of odor and pest problems.) Mix in leaves, grass clippings, twigs, and shredded newspaper in amounts roughly equal to the food waste. Add a little water to start, and then water about once a week to keep everything moist. Every week or two, you should turn or lightly stir the pile. Your compost should be ready to use as fertilizer in about one to four months.

The worst option for disposing of food waste is placing it in a landfill or burning it. These processes result in more greenhouse gases being released into the atmosphere. Be sure your food waste program considers all other hierarchy options before trashing leftovers.

Clean Smart

"Reusable," "biodegradable," and "recycled" are the key words when it comes to cleaning and reducing your carbon footprint. Reusable means using fabric dishcloths and cleaning cloths instead of paper towels to clean. Natural sponges—not synthetic—are also a good choice, as they are biodegradable.

Other biodegradable cleaning supplies can include dishwashing detergent, disinfectant, floor and carpet cleaner, towels, pot scrubbers, mops, and brooms. These items may also be made using recycled materials. And speaking of recycled, if you must use paper towels, be

Students in New Haven, Connecticut, use compost to fertilize their school's organic garden. Nutrients are released into the soil as the food decomposes.

sure to use those made with recycled content. According to Green Seal, a nonprofit environmental advocacy group, using paper towels with 100 percent recycled materials would eliminate approximately one million tons of paper waste annually.

4 | Raise Awareness

Many of the ways you can reduce your carbon footprint at school require you to take action, such as conducting an energy audit in your classroom, volunteering to rake or shovel, or overseeing a food waste program. Other reduction methods, like getting the district to buy energy-efficient appliances or retrofitting school buses, are out of your direct control. The second group of methods depend less on action and more on you speaking up, knowledgeably, about global warming issues. They involve raising awareness.

Believe it or not, raising awareness can make as big a difference in reducing greenhouse gas emissions as any program or activity. In fact, the U.S. Department of Energy has stated that simply raising awareness can result in an energy savings of up to 3 percent for your school. That's because people start to "think green" and make positive changes in their behavior.

Lessons Learned

One way to raise awareness of global warming is to make it part of your school's curriculum, or the courses you study.

An assistant principal in Bullhead City, Arizona, checks out students' solar ovens. School projects that teach about solar energy help you understand how to reduce your carbon footprint.

Many schools now offer courses or class units devoted to the effect of our carbon footprint on the planet. If your school doesn't provide such lessons, you will have to convince them that this is a good idea.

In America, setting curriculum is the job of the state where you live, along with the local school board. They decide what needs to be covered. Specific lessons within the curriculum are created by your teachers. Students normally don't have much contact, if any, with school boards or state administrators. However, they can discuss what they would like to see in the curriculum with teachers. Chances are good that at least a few teachers in your school have an interest in environmental issues. Find out who these teachers are and talk to them about getting lessons on global warming and greenhouse gases into the curriculum.

If your efforts to change the curriculum go nowhere, you might prepare a presentation on reducing carbon emissions instead. This can be a class project, done for extra credit, or something you submit as part of a science fair. At the very least, a presentation on global warming raises awareness.

Join or Start a Club

A single person can make a difference, but a group of like-minded people acting together can bring about even bigger changes. If your school has an environmental club, join it. If there is no such organization, find out how to start one.

School clubs allow members to enjoy a certain activity with people who feel the same way. They are also a way for members to share their knowledge and passion about a subject with the rest of the school. This makes clubs a great outlet for raising awareness of a cause—reducing our carbon footprint, for instance.

Keep in mind that a group of friends getting together to discuss the greenhouse effect is not the same as an official school club. Clubs hold regular meetings, organize events, and expect dedication and action. Some clubs also receive small amounts of money that schools set aside for student organizations and their projects. You want to be part of an organized effort to raise awareness of the dangers of carbon emissions and other pollution.

Start or Expand a School Recycling Program

Creating a recycling program may seem more like an action item than an awareness maneuver. Actually, it's both. When people see recycling

Deciding what you can and should recycle, as well as separating reusable materials by category, are two important steps in the recycling process.

boxes placed strategically around the school—or a bin containing food waste for composting—they can't help but pay attention.

There are several steps to having a successful recycling program:

1. Figure out what you will recycle. Most communities in America are set up to recycle paper, so that's where you should start. Other materials for recycling may include aluminum and plastic (cans and bottles), glass, batteries, and printer/copier ink cartridges.

2. Find a company or organization willing to take the items you collect. Towns and cities may operate their own recycling operations, or you can contact a waste hauler or professional recycling center. Some places will pick up your recyclables, while others require you to bring the materials to them. Some recycling centers even pay, usually pennies on the pound, for recycled material. Earth 911 (http://www.earth911.org) can help you find a recycling

organization near you through a database searchable by zip code or state.

3. Choose collection containers. You'll want boxes and bins that don't take up too much space but are noticeable. Paper is used in every classroom and office, so recycling containers for paper should be widely available. A bin for food waste can be placed either in the school's kitchen, or, if you think your fellow students can be trusted not to make a mess, somewhere near trash bins in the cafeteria.

4. Decide how to best sort and store what you collect. Recycled materials won't be picked up every day, so you'll have to make arrangements to store items until they leave the building. Try to find a spot inside that is relatively dry and clean; the area should be covered if it is outside. Don't let materials pile up and create clutter, and make sure you're not in violation of any fire codes, especially when storing paper. Also, make sure used food containers are cleaned first, or you might have a problem with bugs or larger pests.

5. Educate students, teachers, and staff about your program. Post clear, simple instructions near each bin about what is acceptable to recycle in a particular container. Also, let recyclers know the correct condition of materials to be recycled. For instance, should papers be tied in bundles? Are lids and caps supposed to be removed from bottles? Do cans need to be crushed?

Students in Honolulu, Hawaii, have a great time at the Kokua Festival. The annual event raises awareness and supports environmental education programs in Hawaiian schools.

Publicize and Reward

People need information in order to participate in a successful recycling program. There are various ways to call attention to your carbon footprint–reduction effort and get students and teachers to take part. Some are traditional, and others are just plain fun.

Once you have conducted an energy audit, post the results—in your classroom, on a bulletin board or wall where everyone can see it, or, to save paper, on your school's Web site. Write an article about your experiences as a "green" student and submit it to your school's newspaper or newsletter, or send it to your local newspaper for publication.

You can give a straightforward presentation on global warming at a school assembly, or get a little creative. You and classmates could perform a comedy skit about students who refuse to recycle being attacked by a mound of garbage. (This is only an example. You can come up with even better storylines of your own.) Take pictures of the school's environmental club performing a cleanup, then present the photos as an online or in-school gallery exhibit.

One sure way to get people involved is to offer them something in return. Offer prizes for the person who recycles the most pounds of paper in one month or comes up with the most effective or least expensive way to reduce his or her electricity consumption. Make "thinking green" a competition within your class, between classes, or even among schools in your district. Prizes can be something tangible, like an iPod; a money-equivalent, like a gift certificate for music downloads; or an event, like a pizza party for the winner and a bunch of his or her friends. If you don't have much money for prizes, maybe you can offer a service—for instance, promise to clean someone's locker or do some other heinous chore.

It can take a lot of time and effort to make people aware of global warming or reduce your own personal carbon footprint. The effort is totally worth it, though. If we all conserve energy and take steps to lessen human-made carbon emissions, the world we call home will be a much safer, healthier, and happier place to live.

Glossary

biodegradable Able to decompose through natural means.

biodiesel Renewable fuel made from vegetable oils or animal fat.

black carbon Particulate emission from partially combusted diesel fuel.

carbon footprint A person's individual contribution to higher carbon dioxide levels in the atmosphere.

CO_2 Scientific abbreviation for carbon dioxide.

compost Mix of organic materials that, when it decomposes, can be used as fertilizer.

compressor coils Coils in which gases are compressed to make refrigerators or air conditioners work.

decompose To decay or rot.

emit To release or send out.

energy audit Systematic investigation showing how energy is being used or misused.

fossil fuel Fuel created from the remains of ancient animals and plants.

global warming Slow but steady increase in the temperature of Earth's surface and its oceans due to carbon dioxide and other gases.

graphite Writing material used in pencils, also known as pencil lead.

greenhouse effect Process by which solar energy comes through the atmosphere to warm Earth but gets trapped as heat as it radiates back out into space.

hierarchy Arrangement showing order from greatest to least.

HVAC Abbreviation for heating, ventilation, air-conditioning; indoor climate-control systems.

idle To keep a vehicle's engine running when the vehicle isn't in motion.

incinerate To burn.

infiltrate To enter when it's not expected or desired.

methane Odorless, colorless gas used as fuel; a greenhouse gas.

nitrous oxide An inorganic greenhouse gas.

organic From a living organism. When used regarding food, it means that only natural pesticides and fertilizers were used.

rendering Separating the fats and oils from food waste.

retrofit To place new devices on old machinery in order to make it work better.

For More Information

Alliance to Save Energy
1850 M Street NW, Suite 600
Washington, DC 20036
(202) 857-0666
Web site: http://www.ase.org/section/_audience/consumers/kids
The Alliance to Save Energy is a nonprofit advocacy group that offers information
and educational programs on reducing greenhouse gas emissions and saving
consumers money. The group's site features kids-only pages, including Energy
Hog interactive games.

Clean Air-Cool Planet
100 Market Street, Suite 204
Portsmouth, NH 03801
Web site: http://www.cleanair-coolplanet.org
The nonprofit advocacy group Clean Air-Cool Planet partners with companies,
campuses, communities, and science centers throughout the northeastern United
States and Canada to help people understand global warming and reduce their
carbon emissions.

Natural Resources Canada
615 Booth Street, Room 755
Ottawa, ON K1A 0E9
Canada
Web site: http://www.nrcan.gc.ca/com/index-eng.php

Natural Resources Canada works to ensure the responsible development of Canada's natural resources, offering an up-to-date knowledge base of national resources.

The Office of Energy Efficiency (OEE)
580 Booth Street, 18th Floor
Ottawa, ON K1A 0E4
Canada
Web site: http://oee.nrcan.gc.ca/english
The OEE provides practical energy conservation advice to consumers, school boards, businesses, and institutions, and has links to hundreds of related sites around the world.

U.S. Department of Energy (DOE)
1000 Independence Avenue NW
Washington, DC 20585
Web site: http://www.energy.gov
The mission of the DOE is to advance the national, economic, and energy security of the United States by promoting scientific and technological innovation.

U.S. Environmental Protection Agency (EPA)
Ariel Rios Building
1200 Pennsylvania Avenue NW
Washington, DC 20460
Web site: http://epa.gov
The mission of the Environmental Protection Agency is to protect human health and the environment.

Web Sites

Due to the changing nature of Internet links, Rosen Publishing has developed an online list of Web sites related to the subject of this book. This site is updated regularly. Please use this link to access the list:

http://www.rosenlinks.com/ycf/atsc

For Further Reading

Adams, Richard C., and Robert Gardner. *Energy Projects for Young Scientists*. London, England: Franklin Watts, 2003.

Campbell, Stu. *Let It Rot! The Gardener's Guide to Composting*. 3rd ed. North Adams, MA: Storey Publishing, 1998.

Gore, Al. *An Inconvenient Truth: The Crisis of Global Warming (Adapted for a New Generation)*. New York, NY: Viking, 2006.

Hocking, Colin. *Global Warming and the Greenhouse Effect*. Berkeley, CA: University of California Press, 2002.

Nikel-Zueger, Manuel. *Critical Thinking About Environmental Issues: Energy*. Farmington Hills, MI: Greenhaven Press, 2003.

Silverstein, Alan. *Global Warming*. Kirkland, WA: 21st Century, 2003.

Stille, Darlene R. *The Greenhouse Effect: Warming the Planet*. Mankato, MN: Compass Point Books, 2006.

Young, Mitchell. *Garbage and Recycling*. Farmington Hills, MI: Greenhaven Press, 2007.

Bibliography

Alliance to Save Energy. "Student Energy Auditor Training: How to Save Energy at Your School." 2007. Retrieved December 2007 (http://www.ase.org/uploaded_files/greenschools/background.pdf).

California Integrated Waste Management Board. "The Worm Guide: A Vericomposting Guide for Teachers." June 2004. Retrieved December 2007 (http://www.ciwmb.ca.gov/Publications/Schools/56001007.pdf).

Clean Air Task Force. "Diesel Background and Highlights." 2007. Retrieved December 2007 (http://www.catf.us/projects/diesel/background.php).

Environmental Defense. "Clearing the Air on Climate Change." July 2002. Retrieved November 2007 (http://www.environmentaldefense.org/documents/2209_CarEmissionsFactSheet.pdf).

The Jonah Center for Earth and Art. "What Is Eco-Friendly Landscaping?" Retrieved November 2007 (http://thejonahcenter.org/pdf/ecofriendlylandscaping.pdf).

Malik Chua, Jasmin. "TreeHugger Goes Back to School." TreeHugger.com. August 2007. Retrieved December 2007 (http://www.treehugger.com/files/2007/08/back_to_school.php).

National Association of Independent Schools. "101 Ways to Go Global and Green." Retrieved November 2007 (http://www.nais.org/resources/index.cfm?ItemNumber=149283).

National Park Service. "How You Can Help Reduce Greenhouse Gas Emissions Through Transportation Choices." July 2007. Retrieved December 2007 (http://www.nps.gov/pore/naturescience/climatechange_action_transportation.htm).

Recycling Association of Minnesota. "Buy Recycled: Seven Ways Your School Can Help Save the Environment and Save Money at the Same Time." November 2002. Retrieved December 2007 (http://www.p2pays.org/ref/26/25292/25292.pdf).

Rycroft, Nicole. "Printing's Climate Impact." Print Action Online. 2005. Retrieved December 2007 (http://www.printaction.com/default.php/magazine/december06_rycroft).

Texas Commission on Environmental Quality. "Diesel Exhaust and School Bus Idling: What You Should Know." September 2007. Retrieved December 2007 (http://www.tceq.state.tx.us/files/gi-374.pdf_4141304.pdf).

TrailLink. "The Short Trip with Big Impacts: Walking, Biking, and Climate Change." 2007. Retrieved January 9, 2008 (http://www.railtrails.org/resources/documents/whatwedo/TrailLink%2007%20Program_Climate.pdf.).

TreeHugger.com. "Cleaner School Bus Fuel in Chicago." Retrieved December 2007 (http://www.treehugger.com/files/2005/10/chicago_has_cer.php).

TreeHugger.com. "How to Green Your Cleaning." January 2007. Retrieved December 2007 (http://www.treehugger.com/files/2007/01/|how_to_green_your_cleaning.php).

U.S. Environmental Protection Agency. "Basic Information About Food Scraps." November 2007. Retrieved December 2007 (http://www.epa.gov/epaoswer/non-hw/organics/fd-basic.htm).

U.S. Environmental Protection Agency. "Beneficial Landscaping." August 2006. Retrieved November 2007 (http://www.epa.gov/greenkit/landscap.htm).

U.S. Environmental Protection Agency. "Clean School Bus USA."
     October 2007. Retrieved December 2007 (http://www.epa.gov/
     cleanschoolbus).

Wortman, David. "Eco Checklist 2007: Green Gear for the Back-to-
     School Blues." July 2007. Retrieved December 2007 (http://www.
     thegreenguide.com/doc/121/backtoschool).

Index

A

America's Second Harvest, 27
appliances, energy-efficient, 23, 25, 31

B

biodiesel fuel, 10–11, 28
"black carbon," 9

C

carbon dioxide, 4, 5, 7, 8, 13, 14, 22
carbon filtering, 10
carbon footprint, definition of, 5
car pool, 8
clubs, joining or starting, 33
coal, 6, 14
compact fluorescent lightbulbs, 17
composting, 29

D

diesel oxidation catalysts, 10

E

Earth 911, 34
electricity, generation of, 14
energy audits, 15–16, 31, 36

F

Farm to School program, 24
food cycle, 22–24
food waste programs, 26–29, 31
fossil fuels, 6, 8, 14, 16, 22, 24

G

global warming, 4, 31, 32, 37
Gore, Al, 4, 5
greenhouse effect, 4
greenhouse gases, 4, 6, 11, 14, 24, 29, 31

L

landscaping/groundskeeping, 11–13

N

National Hunger Clearinghouse, 27
native vegetation, use of, 11–13
natural gas, 14, 16

O

oil, 6, 14, 16

P

paper, recycling/purchasing of, 18–20
petroleum, 6
public transportation, 8

R

recycling program, starting or expanding, 33–37
rendering, 28

S

school buses, 8–10
    and alternative fuels, 10–11
    and better driving practices, 11
    retrofitting, 10, 31

About the Author

Jeanne Nagle is a writer and editor in upstate New York. She has a longstanding interest in environmental issues and is a member of Care of God's Creation, a grassroots environmental group in her area. Among her many titles written for Rosen Publishing is *Smart Shopping: Shopping Green*.

Photo Credits

Cover (top) © www.istockphoto.com/Frank van den Bergh; cover (middle), pp. 6, 8 Shutterstock.com; cover (bottom), pp. 9, 17, 28, 32 © AP Images; p. 12 © Kathy McLaughlin/The Image Works; p. 15 © David R. Frazier/The Image Works; pp. 14, 19 © Donovan Reese/Stone/Getty Images; p. 21 © www.istockphoto.com/Yiap See Fat; p. 23 © www.istockphoto.com/Dr. Heinz Linke; p. 30 © Peter Hvzdak/The Image Works; p. 34 © Syracuse Newspapers/David Lassman/The Image Works; pp. 31, 36 © Tim Mosenfelder/Getty Images.

Designer: Les Kanturek; Editor: Christopher Roberts; Photo Researcher: Marty Levick